Tunisian

Easy Patterns to Start

Table of Contents

Crochet For Beginners

Introduction

Hello and welcome to the world of crocheting! You'll learn how to make lots of different things and move towards making your own designs. You can use crocheting for a bunch of different reasons. Some people even go on to sell the things they crochet. All you need to do something like that is a little help. If you want to create personal presents, sell your creations, or just make something for yourself, then this is for you.

Lots of people crochet and now you're about to become one of them. So read on a little more, familiarize yourself with what you need, and move on to crocheting your own handmade goods.

Chapter 1 – The Basics of Crocheting

There are three basic things you need to start crocheting. You need a packet of hooks, some yarn, and of course you need a pattern. Patterns come in different categories of difficulty from beginner, easy, intermediate, and hard. As a beginner you want to start with a really basic beginner one. As you practice you can move up and work from harder patterns. Eventually you'll be able to create your own patterns.

When you take a look at a pattern for the first time you might be a little intimidated. They use special crocheting terms you won't understand at first. They can also be more than you expected and difficult to read as a beginner. That's the point of a guide like this. To introduce you to these terms and teach you how to read patterns in the first place. You have to be able to do that before you can do anything else after all. So let's take a look at some of the basics of crochet patterns.

It's important to remember that crochet patterns show you rows or rounds. Rounds are commonly abbreviated to rnds as well. When you see rnds it means how many rounds there are. The pattern will also tell you whether you're dealing with rounds, rows, or both.

Another very basic step that shouldn't be overlooked is always counting your stitches. If you're even one stitch out things can go wrong pretty quick and ruin a lot of hard work. What's also important to check is the gauge. A gauge tells you how long a set of stitches should be. It's unique to the pattern you're using so do the stitches and measure it up. If it's too big then use a smaller hook. Conversely you need to use a bigger hook if the gauge is too small.

Of course if you read this guide cover to cover and you still don't fully grasp it you may want to consider getting lessons. This guide should be more than enough but some people do have difficulty learning from guides and need a more hands on approach.

There will be a glossary at the end of this book for all the different terms and symbols you're likely to encounter while crocheting so don't be afraid of them. Just look them up a little further on.

Now that you're familiar with the way patterns work let's take a look at a very basic one. We need to learn how to read them after all.

Row 1: (remember patterns are written in rows or rounds!) With a size H hook, ch 15, sc in 2nd ch from hook and in each ch across, turn.

(14 sc)

Oh wow that definitely looks scary doesn't it? Let's translate it to basic English so we know what it actually means.

Row 1: Use a size H crochet hook to make 15 chain stitches, single cross in the second chain stitch from the hook, and turn each chain stich across. The bit at the end lets you know there are 14 single crochets at the end of the row.

Now that sounds a little better, but still confusing. So let's take a look at slip knots, chain stitches, and everything inbetween.

Chapter 2 – Stitching Basics

Now you know how to read a crochet pattern it's time to learn what all that meant and how to do what the pattern tells you. Don't worry about how to hold the crochet needle in the first place. There are a few ways to do it so find a way that works best for you. A popular method of holding it is to simply hold it like a pencil. So what about chain stitches? Let's take a look.

In order to start a chain stitch, or indeed any stitch, you need a slip knot. A slip knot is typically the first part of any crocheting pattern. From there you move to chain stitches that form the base for the pattern and are what you work from. A chain stitch is represented in a pattern by the simple abbreviation "ch". So when you see that in a pattern it's an indication you need to chain stitch.

Making a slip knot and turning it into a chain stitch is pretty simple. Start by making a loop in the yarn about six inches away from the yarn. The end of the yarn still attached to the ball is known as the "yarn end". The "free end", or the actual end of your yarn, needs to be behind the yarn end in the loop. Then you just insert your hook into the loop and hook the free end on to the end of your hook. After that you pull that end through the loop, forming a knot around the working area (the thick bit near the hook) of your crochet hook. Then simply pull on the yarn end to close and tighten the hook. There should still be some wiggle room left but there you have it; you've created your very first slip knot!

Now hold the hook with your left hand, taking hold of the base of the knot with your thumb and index finger. Then bring yarn over the hook from back to front, hooking it, and then draw the hooked yarn through the loop of the slip knot and up on to the working area. Congratulations on making your first chain stitch. Keep doing this as many times as the pattern indicates, keeping a firm grip on the slip knot and adjusting every few stitches to keep everything in place. You'll need to practice at first so just keep going until you're comfortable making chain stitches. They are the most vital first step after all and necessary for any pattern to succeed. Don't worry if your stitches aren't perfect. They will be soon.

When you can make six chains in a row without a mistake it's time to move on to the next step. One important thing to remember is that the initial slipknot, and the knot on the hook, are not classed as parts of the chain. So when you count the chain stitches (which we established is important) keep this in mind and count properly. You'll also almost never work into the first stitch in a chain. The pattern will tell you how many chains you need to skip before you start working, so pay close attention to that too. To work a chain insert the hook through the center of the v shape (your stitches should look like V's). You're going to work every stitch in the chain unless, again, the pattern says otherwise. You should also never work the initial slip knot. Take care to not skip the last chain at the end either.

Chapter 3 – Crochet Basics

One of the basic stitches is called the single crochet, and is represented in a pattern by the abbreviation sc. There is also the double stitch and lots of other stitches, but we're focusing on the most basic one right now.

To perform a basic single crochet make a slip knot and then chain six, as we learned how to do in the previous chapter. Then put the hook through the second chain and bring the yarn over the hook from back to front. Draw the yarn through the chain and on to the working area of the hook, giving you two loops on the hook. Bring the yarn back through the hook from back to front again and draw it through both hoops on the hook. If you do it properly you'll still have a loop on the hook and you'll have done a single crochet. You then move on to the next chain and repeat the steps; hooking the yarn from back to front and drawing it through the chain stitch. You "yarn over" (a term that means bringing the yarn over the hook from back to front) once more and draw it through both loops. Do this for every chain, making sure to do the last one, and you'll have completed your first row of single crochets. Make sure to keep the cross stitch facing the right way too. The v's should always face you.

Now you've done one row it's time to turn the work clockwise, without dropping the crochet hook, and begin on working your way back. That's how you do the second row and is what is meant by turning in crochet patterns. Another difference between the second row and the first is that you work into the previous row, rather than the initial chain. This is also true for any rows after the second one. Bring the hook through the last stitch of the previous row, under the top two loops, and bring the yarn over the hook from the back to the front. Draw the yarn through the stitch and on to the working area of the hook to form two loops, as you did in the previous step. Then you bring the yarn from back to front once more, through the loops, and continue on like you did before; going through each stitch and being careful to not forget the last one. When you get to the end you should have two rows of five single stitches.

In order to fasten off, or finish your work, you need to cut the yarn, leaving a six inch stretch at the end. Draw the hook up, drawing the cut yarn through the stitch. Then just pull the six inch end to close the stitch and finish your work. Now that you know about the single crochet it's time to learn about the double crochet.

Making a double crochet is similar to making a single one. The first major difference is to chain 14 rather than the six you did with single crochets. You also need to skip the first three chains, inserting the hook in the fourth chain, rather than the second. From there things are pretty similar to how you remember them. Bring the yarn over the hook and draw it through the stitch and on to the hook to form three loops on the crochet hook. Then bring the yarn over the hook and through the first two loops on the hook. You'll now have two loops left on the hook. Draw the yarn over one more time, inserting it through both remaining hooks, and you'll end up with one loop left. That's the first double crochet down. Keep doing this until you've done all your double stitches. When you're done count how many you have. There should be twelve, as the first three you skipped at the start will have become a double stitch by this point.

In order to raise the hook and begin the second chain you need to stich three. This is known as the turning chain. It also forms the first double stitch so begin the second row from the second stitch, rather than the first. Be sure to insert the hook through the top two loops to do this correctly. Just keep going like you did before in order to finish the second row and however many you need to do after that.

Fastening off with a double crochet is the same as it is for a single crochet. Cut the yarn with six inches left, draw it through the stitch, and pull it to close the stitch. Now you have the single and double crochet down it's time to look at some other stitches.

Chapter 4 – Advanced Crochets

There are a multitude of advanced crocheting stitches. Far too many for one little guide like this to take care of. If you encounter a stitch type you aren't sure of look it up to get a good idea. We're covering the basics here and getting you started. So let's move on to some more advanced stitches that are still basic. We'll begin with the half double crochet.

The half double crochet is represented in a pattern by hdc, and is takes out one of the steps in making a double crochet. It leaves you with something that's about half as tall as a regular double crochet.

The first step with the double crochet is to make a slip knot and chain 13. Bring the yarn over the crochet hook from back to front once and insert the hook in the third chain, skipping the first two. Bring the yarn up over crochet hook, drawing it through the chain and on to the hook. You should have three loops on the hook like you did with the double crochet. Bring more yarn over the hook and draw it through all three loops. That's all you need to do a double crochet. There should be one loop left on the hook. Keep going across the row of stitches until you get to the end. There should be twelve half double crochets by the time you're done.

This time when you chain to turn the work, you need to chain two, rather than three. The turning chain also counts as the first crochet, so begin working your way back across from the second stitch rather than the first. Also be sure to insert the hook under the top two loops of the stitch. Work your way back across the stitch until you get to the end of the second row and you're done. Follow the same fastening off procedure as before when you've practiced enough or when you've finished the pattern.

The last kind of crochet we're going to look at is the treble crochet. It's like the other crochets we've done so far. Start by making your slip knot and this time cross stitching fifteen. Then you wrap the yarn around the hook from back to front twice, and insert the hook into the fifth chain. Bring the yarn over the hook, drawing it through the chain and onto the hook as before. This time there should be four loops on the hook. Bring the yarn over the hook again and pull it through the first two loops, leaving you with three loops on the hook. Bring the yarn over once again, this time through the next two loops, leaving you with two. Bring the yarn through both loops one last time, leaving you with one loop and a complete treble crochet.

In order to work on another row you need to raise the yarn again. This time to raise the yarn you stitch four for the turning chain. They also count as the first treble crochet on the new row, so start from the second chain and work your way across. Each row should have twelve stitches when you're done. Then it's time to fasten off using the same technique you've been using before.

Chapter 5 – Slip Stitches And Other Advanced Techniques

Now that you know the basic crochets it's time to learn a stitch. We'll take a look at the slip stitch, represented in a pattern as sl st. The slip stitch is the shortest of the stitches and is really more a technique to get yarn across stitches without adding height. They can also be used to join your work together when you're working on a round, rather than a row. As you can see it's a handy trick to know and vital to crocheting.

You start by chaining ten and from there move on to using double crochet from the fourth chain. Now instead of raising the yarn up to work row two we'll just slip across. Now chain one, instead of the three you usually do for the turning chain with a double crochet. It doesn't count as stitch so you need to insert the hook under the loops of the first stitch, then draw the yarn through both loops of the stitch and loop on the hook. That's one slip stitch down. Now repeat that for the first three stitches and then raise the yarn by stitching three to finish the rest of the row with a double stitch. You can see how the second row is slightly smaller than the first one because you slipped past the first three crochets. Now that you know how to do a slip stitch we'll look at how to use one to turn a chain into a circle. It's a nifty little trick that opens up a lot of possibilities with crocheting. It's a technique employed a lot in making hats for example.

Start by first of all chaining six. Then insert the crochet hook through the first chain next to the slip knot and, after yarning over, draw the yarn through the chain and the loop on the hook. You just turned six stitches into a circle. Moving on from forming a circle we can use the slip stitch to join the end of one round to the beginning. It sounds a little complicated but you aren't doing anything you haven't done before.

Start by making a ring like you did before. Stitch six and join them together with a slip stitch. Then you chain three, like you do to raise the yarn, and then double crochet eleven into the center of the ring. When you've done that insert your crochet hook into beginning chain three. Yarn over as usual and then draw it through the chain and loop on the hook to join the round of double crochets. You can see how something like that can come in handy and it can be done with any kinds of crochets and loops.

By now you've undoubtedly used a lot of yarn, and have probably even ran out on more than one occasion. You can't have that happening while you're working a pattern though, can you? So what do you do when you're running out of yarn but aren't finished? Let's take a look at how to replace the yarn when crocheting.

It's easiest to bring in the new yarn at the end of a row. It's possible to do it in the middle of one but it's more difficult. In order to change the yarn at the end of a row you need to work the last stitch with your old yarn until you have two loops left on the hook. Then you introduce the new yarn and use it to finish the stitch and complete the row. You can then turn the stitch and keep going with your new yarn.

If you aren't careful and you have to use the new yarn in the middle of a stitch you can still do that. In that case what you do is work as many stitches as you can with the old yarn. When you know you don't have enough left you can complete a stitch with new yarn as explained before. It's just easier to do it at the end of a row rather than in the middle of one.

Another advanced technique is what is known as crocheting in the front and back loops, represented as front lp or back lp in a pattern. Normally when you crochet you work with both loops. By working with just one you leave a horizontal bar and the fabric becomes a bit more elasticated than it would usually be. When you work a stitch you usually put the hook through the front of the chain and through the center of the V, as explained before. The goes under the bar of the stitch on the way out too. This causes it to go below the front and back loops.

To work just the back loop insert the hook under just the back loop. It's as simple as that. Working the front loop is done by putting the hook under just the front loop. Work from there as the pattern indicates and you'll have worked with just the front or back loop. Well done you.

Now that you know enough to be getting on with it's time to look at some introductory patterns to get you started. You should know enough to do these patterns. If you run into a word or term you don't understand then refer to the glossary at the end of the book to double check the meaning. Good luck!

Chapter 6 – Patterns For You To Try

The first pattern we'll be looking at is a pretty easy one. It's for a simple soap holder. Getting tired of little bits of soap getting everywhere? Now you can make your own little holder. Crocheting really can be used to make all manner of things. So let's look at the pattern. Remember, it might sound daunting but once you know what it means it becomes pretty easy.

What you need;

- *A size I crochet hook*

- *A size H crochet hook*

- *35 yards of yarn in one color*

- *1 yard of yarn in another color*

- *A yarn needle*

A list of abbreviations used in this pattern;

Sl st – slip stitch

St(s) – stitch(es)

Ch- chain

Sc- single crochet

Dc- double crochet

Hdc- half double crochet

t-ch turning chain

As you can see this is all stuff we've covered and become familiar with.

Gauge; four stitches and three rows should be 1 inches

A quick note is that Row 3/round 3 is a row that becomes a round. You need to crochet all the way across the row and then work your way down the side, across the bottom, and then up the other side to turn it all into a round.

Now for the instructions;

With I hook

Ch 11

Row 1: Sc in 2nd ch from hook, and in each ch across. Turn. (10)

Row 2: Ch 1, sc in each st across. Turn. (10)

Row 3/round 3: Ch 1, 2 sc in the first st, sc in each st until the last st of the row, 2 sc in the last st of the row. Work 3 sc down the side of the rows. Working in the bottom loops of the original chain, 2 sc in first ch, sc in each ch until the last ch, 2 sc in the last ch. Work 3 sc up the side of the rows. Join in the first sc. Don't turn. You'll now be working in the round (30)

Round 4: Ch 4 (counts as dc and ch 1), sk next st *dc in next st, ch 1, sk next st** repeat from * to ** around. Join in top of t-ch (15 dcs)

Round 5: ch 4 (counts as dc and ch 1), *dc in ch-1 sp, ch 1** Repeat from * to ** around. Join in top of t-ch (15 dcs)

Rounds 6-9: Repeat round 5

Round 10: ch 1, hdc in each ch-1 sp and dc around. Fasten off, join using an invisible join. (30)

You make the drawstring for the bag using the H hook and by following these instructions;

Tightly chain 70. Fasten off and leave a long tail. Use the yarn needle to thread the end of the drawstring through and weave it through the hdc sts in round 10. Knot and trim ends.

Congratulations on finishing your first crochet project! Let's take a look at another pattern now we've got a feel for them.

Pink and Red Crochet Hearts

These lovely little hearts are an ideal valentines present, and they aren't that difficult to make.

You will need;

1 skein of weighted yarn

E crochet hook

Your gauge is that 7 stitches should be 1 inch and 2 and a half rows also equal one inch.

Instructions;

The small heart should be about 3 and a half inches tall and three and a half inches across. The larger heart is about 4 inches by 4 inches.

Small heart;

Round 1: (RS) Ch 5, sl st into 1st ch to create loop, ch 2, 19 dcs into loop sl st into top of 1st dc, do not turn throughout

Round 2: Ch 1, 2 scs into next 2 sts, 1 hdc into next 3 sts, 1 dc in next 4 sts, 3 dcs into next st (creates bottom tip of heart), 1 dc into next 4 sts, 1 hdc into next 3 sts, 2 scs in next 2 sts, sl st to 1st sc (25 sts)

Round 3: Ch 1, 1 sc in same st, 2 hdcs in next st, 1 dc in next 4 sts, 1 hdc in next 2 sts, 1 sc in next 4 sts, 3 scs in next st (should be in the middle sc of 3-sc tip of row below), 1 sc in next 4 sts, 1 hdc in next 2 sts, 1 dc in next 4 sts, 2 hdcs in next st, 1 sc in next st, sl st to 1st sc (29 sts)

Round 4: Ch 1, 1 sc in same st, 1 dc in next st, 2 dcs in next 4 sts, 1 sc in next 8 sts, 3 scs in next st (again, should be in the tip), 1 sc in next 8 sts, 2 dcs in next 4 sts, 1 dc in next st, 1 sc in next st, sl st to 1st sc (39 sts)

Round 5: Ch 1, 1 sc in same st, 2 dcs in next 3 sts, 1 dc in next st, 2 dcs in next st, 1 dc in next st, 1 hdc in next 4 sts, 2 scs in next st, 1 sc in next 7 sts, 3 scs in next st (again, should be the tip), 1 sc in next 7 sts, 2 scs in next st, 1 hdc in next 4 sts, 1 dc in next st, 2 dcs in next st, 1 dc in next st, 2 dcs in next 3 sts, 1 sc in next st, sl st to 1st sc (51 sts)

Fasten off here for small heart; add one more round, featured below, for the larger heart.

Round 6: Ch 1, 1 sc in same st, 2 dcs in next st, 1 dc in next 3 sts, 2 dcs in next st, 1 dc in next 2 sts, 2 dcs in next st, 1 dc in next 3 sts, 2 dcs in next st, 1 hdc in next 4 sts, 1 sc in next 8 sts, 3 scs in next st (tip), 1 sc in next 8 sts, 1 hdc in next 4 sts, 2 dcs in next st, 1 dc in next 3 sts, 2 dcs in next st, 1 dc in next 2 sts, 2 dcs in next st, 1 dc in next 3 sts, 2 dcs in next st, 1 sc in last st, sl st to 1st st (61 sts), fasten off.

You can find tons of crocheting patterns online or in magazines. Remember to make sure to stick to things that are at your level. Though don't be afraid to try something tougher when you feel that you're ready.

Chapter 7 – Glossary

Crochet patterns can be very confusing because they rely on simplified terminology and abbreviations. For the sake of your sanity here is a list of the commonly used terms in crochet patterns.

Beg means begin/beginning

Bpdc means back post double crochet

Bpsc means back post single crochet

Bptr means back post treble crochet

CC means contrasting color

Ch means chain stitch

Ch refers to chain or space previously made (i.e. ch-1 space)

ch sp means chain space

cl means cluster

cm means centimeter(s)

dc means double crochet

dc dec means double crochet 2 or more stitches together, as indicated

dec means decrease/decreases/decreasing

dtr means double treble crochet

fpdc means front post double crochet

fpsc means front post single crochet

fptr means front post treble crochet

g means grams

hdc means half double crochet

hdc dec means half double crochet (decrease) 2 or more stitches together, as indicated

inc means increase/increases/increasing

lp(s means loops(s)

MC means main color

Mm means millimeter(s)

Oz means ounce(s)

Pc means popcorn

Rem means remain/remaining

Rep means repeat(s)

rnd(s means round(s)

RS means right side

Sc means single crochet

sc dec means single crochet (decrease) 2 or more stitches together, as indicated

sk means skip(ped)

sl st means slip stitch

sp(s means space(s)

st(s means stitch(es)

tog means together

tr means treble crochet

trtr means triple treble

WS means wrong side

yd(s) means yard(s)

yo means yarn over

You're also going to encounter symbols that mean different things. Here's a look at what symbols mean in crochet patterns.

Parentheses ( ) are used to show a collective group of stitches that need to be worked in one go, in one place. So just follow them how they say, where they say.

Brackets [ ] show that instructions are to be repeated. So do what is inside the brackets how many times it says you have to.

Braces { } are used as a combination of brackets and parentheses. They show a set of instructions that is to be repeated, or to show multiple repetitions.

Asterisks, both * and ** are used to show repetition.

They can be confusing at first but you'll soon get a good grasp on them.

Conclusion

Well there you have it. You're now prepared to crochet your way out of a wet paper bag, and then make a wet paper bag out of yarn with crocheting. This is what you need to get you started. Feel free to look up more advanced patterns and remember that practice will always make perfect. If at first you don't succeed try and try again. Good luck with your crocheting and never, ever, give up.

Tunisian Crochet Guide for Beginners

Introduction

The Tunisian crochet stitch is known by a few names: The Afghan join, Hook, Railroad Knitting, Shepherd's sewing, weaving, and tricot sew.

Unless you have a customary Tunisian crochet hook, which is a long handed sew snare, then Tunisian sew is truly reasonable for making littler things, for example, wallets, headbands, belts, and other little things which don't require more than twelve join over the column. That is on account of the considerable number of lines keep focused snare, and any more than that, they will tumble off the back end of the snare!

Tunisian Crochet has a long, however discontinuous history; which is the one reasons why it isn't too referred to and famous as weaving and exemplary sew. Most students of history trust that shepherds in the fields made this kind of embroidery, however nobody has discovered surviving confirmation to plainly characterize "when" it was made. The principal "current" appearance of Tunisian Crochet is amid the Victorian Era when distributers started to tap the embroidery market. Lamentably, everybody was calling it something other than what's expected: every distributer had their picked name for the embroidery and they each had their own particular picked line titles. Towards the end of the nineteenth century, even topographical territories had an alternate name for this style of embroidery. The French are credited for calling it Tunisian Crochet, despite the fact that there is no proof to recommend it was begun in Tunis. I haven't discovered the accurate date when Americans started calling it the Afghan Stitch, however the new name was settled by the 1930's.

Tunisian Crochet was well known for the Victorian Era, however for obscure reasons that prominence melted away in the early party of the twentieth Century. There is confirmation of a resurgence of Tunisian Crochet in the late 1960's through the mid 1970's; on the other hand beginning in the mid to late 1980's. After that, Tunisian Crochet has gained enduring ground towards accomplishing the same ubiquity as sewing and exemplary knit. One component keeping Tunisian Crochet down is the fear of distributers to purchase more intricate undertaking examples that utilization Tunisian Crochet; that is evolving... day by day.

Today's fashioners appear to have some kind of uneasy indecision towards Tunisian Crochet. What to call the style of embroidery; what to call the join utilized; how to compose fasten documentations and headings for forming. Previously, these were genuine concerns; in any case, it has been my experience that today's Tunisian Crochet Enthusiast is usual to the perplexity. They know not all the line directions to plainly recognize the mechanics for every line utilized in any case what title the distributer connects to the join.

Chapter 1 – Start with Tunisian Simple Stitch

Tunisian crochet makes a tight fix of woven yarn. It helps in the event that you as of now have a moderate level of solace with standard stitch before leaving on this procedure, however broad sew information is a bit much. The most imperative thing to learn is the Tunisian basic join, yet there are different methods, similar to the Tunisian twofold knit, that can likewise prove to be useful.

Design a Foundation Chain

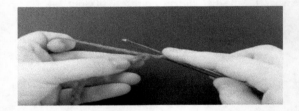

- Join the yarn to your snare utilizing a slipknot, then work an establishment of 10 standard chain lines.

- You can change this number of chains as indicated by your needs. This illustration utilizes 10 chain join, however you ought to modify this number in view of your design's directions or on the fancied length of your work.

Make a Slip Knot

- Make a loop or circle, passing the last part of the yarn underneath the appended side.

- Push the appended side of the yarn up through the circle's base, making a second circle all the while. Fix the first circle around it.

- Embed your knit guide into the second circle. Pull on the last part of the yarn to fix the second circle onto the snare and finish the bunch.

Make a Chain Stitch

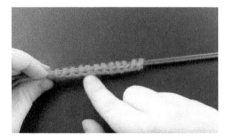

- Yarn over the snare's tip once.

- Pull this yarn-over through the circle as of now on your snare. This finishes one chain fasten.

Insert the hook into the second chain from the hook

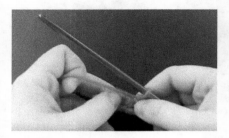

- Yarn over the snare once, then force a circle back through to the front of your piece.

- You can either work your lines into the back circles of your establishment chain or into both the front and back circles. Regardless of which system you utilize, on the other hand, you ought to keep on utilizing the same technique all through the whole work.

- Toward the end of this stride, you ought to have two circles on your snare.

- Note that you are starting your first forward pass. You are additionally making a planning line for whatever is left of your work.

Repeat with the Chain

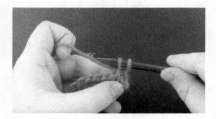

- Take after the same method to draw up a circle through every chain. Proceed until you achieve the end of your establishment chain.

- For every chain, embed the guide into the chain, yarn over the tip, and step the circle back through to the front of the stitch.

- Before the end of this procedure, you ought to have the same number of circles on your snare as you had fastens in your establishment chain. For this case, you will have 10 circles.

- This finishes your first forward pass.

Start Return Pass

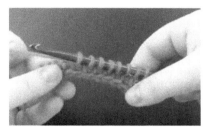

- Yarn over the snare's tip, then force this yarn over through one circle on your snare.

- You ought to still have the same number of circles on your snare as some time recently. For this case, you will have 10 circles.

- This is the first fasten in your arrival pass. The rest are comparative, however, not exactly like it.

- Work a second return pass. Yarn over the snare's tip once more. This time, pull the yarn-over through two circles on your snare.

- After this stride, you will have one less circle on your snare. For this sample, you must have nine circles.

Repeat in Reverse

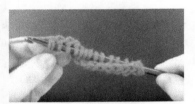

- Repeat the past stride until you achieve the starting point of your work and just have on circle left on your snare.

- For every join, you ought to yarn over the snare and draw the yarn-over through two circles already on the snare.

- Toward the end of every stitch, you will be left with one less circle on your snare.

- Try not to pull through the keep going circle on your snare.

- This stride finishes your first turn around pass. It likewise finishes your preparation row.

- Forward like before. To begin another line of Tunisian knit utilizing the basic join, you should work another forward go in the same fundamental way as the first.

- For this forward pass, embed the snare from right to left into the second vertical bar from the snare. Try not to embed the guide into the vertical bar specifically beneath it; you must utilize the second vertical bar.

- Yarn over the snare's tip and draw it back through to the vertical's front bar. You ought to have two circles on your snare.

- Insert the hook into the next bar, yarn over, and pull it through, giving you three circles on your snare.

- Repeat it, until you have come to the last vertical bar. Try not to work a line into the last vertical bar yet.

Insert the hook into the last two lines of the column

- Find the even bar straightforwardly right of the last vertical bar. After that insert the hook under this flat bar, and also the last vertical bar. Yarn over and pull a circle back through these two fastens to finish your forward pass.

- Note that this stride is just discretionary. On the off chance that coveted, you can essentially draw a circle up from underneath the vertical bar just and reject the flat bar. Utilizing both add soundness to your work, in any case.

- Toward the end of this step, you ought to have 10 circles on your snare, or numerous circles as you had in the foundation chain.

Return Pass

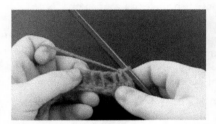

- Complete another return pass line in the same route as the first.

- Yarn over the tip of the snare. Pull this yarn-over through one circle already on the hook.

- Yarn over the snare once more, yet this time, pull it through two circles on your snare. This ought to diminish the quantity of circles on the hook by one. Rehash this progression over whatever remains of the column until there is stand out circle left on the hook.

Repeat the process

- Substitute forward and backward between forward pass and turn around pass columns, finishing at the determination of a converse pass line, until you achieve the end of your straightforward line segment or the end of your general work.

- You can make a whole work utilizing only the Tunisian basic line. You could likewise join the straightforward fasten with different strategies, however, similar to the Tunisian twofold knit.

- On the off chance that you wish to end with just the Tunisian basic line, skip down to the area on completing the Work.

Chapter 2 – Easy Steps of Tunisian Double Crochet

Now, it's time to learn Tunisian double crochet. Follow the following easy to follow steps:

Make a foundation row using Tunisian simple stitch

- The Tunisian twofold sew begins after you have finished an arrangement line utilizing the Tunisian simple line.

- You can work the Tunisian twofold sew into bigger bit of Tunisian basic fastens. The arrangement line is a base begin, yet not a most extreme begin.

- Verify that you have finished an opposite go before you begin the Tunisian twofold sew. There need to just be one circle on your hook when you begin.

Chain two

- Work two standard chain fastens from the circle on your snare.

- These chain fastens will suit the height of Tunisian double crochet row.

Forward pass into the next vertical bar

- Yarn over your hook again, then insert it into the second vertical bar. Yarn over once more, then step this yarn-over back through to the front of your work, making a circle. Yarn over again, then draw your last yarn-over through two circles on the hook.

- Note that the first vertical bar needs to be skirted, as finished with the basic join.

- Leave the last circle of the line on your snare. There ought to as of now be one circle on your snare from before that, then again, giving you a sum of two circles on the snare toward the end of this first double stitch.

- The contrast between the Tunisian simple stitch as well as the Tunisian twofold knit lies completely in this forward pass some portion of the procedure.

Work across the row

- Repeat the past step, working into every vertical stitch of the past until you achieve the end of that past column.

- For each stitch, yarn over the hook, after that insert it into the following vertical bar, and yarn over once more. Move the yarn-over back through to the front, yarn over once more, and draw this last yarn-over through two circles on your snare.

- For the last vertical bar, embed the guide into the level line misleading the privilege of the vertical bar and additionally the vertical bar itself. At the point when pulling a circle back through to the front of the work, verify that you pull it through both bars once more. This adds steadiness to the edge of the work.

- When you achieve the end of your forward pass column, you ought to have 10 circles on your snare, or the quantity of join you began with in your establishment chain.

Reverse pass through stitch

- Yarn over the tip of the snare and draw that yarn-over through one circle beforehand on your stitch.

- Note that the pass go for the Tunisian twofold sew is precisely the same the opposite go for the Tunisian basic fasten.

- Converse go through whatever is left of the line of course. Yarn over the snare, then draw that yarn over through two circles on the stitch.

- You need to be left with one less circle on your hook toward the end of the stitch.

- Repeat this step until one and only circle stays on your hook.

Repeat the process

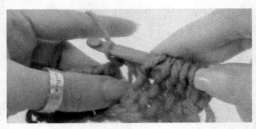

- Exchange forward and backward between the forward pass and switch go until you achieve the end of your Tunisian twofold sew area or the end of your role in general.

- Continuously end with the decision of a reverse pass.

- Skip down to the area on "Completing the Work" in the event that you are prepared to tie off the work toward the culmination of this step.

-

Chapter 3 – Popular Tunisian Crochet Patters for Men

Man crafts are dependably enjoyable to make, yet can in some cases be hard to discover. Female sew examples are anything but difficult to discover; there's ribbon, laces, and blooms all around you look. In any case, sew is not only for young ladies! Trust it or not, folks acknowledge hand crafted knitted examples, as well.

Sew designs for men can be difficult to find and that is the reason we've gathered our most loved free examples all in one spot for you to appreciate. Every one of these examples would make an amazing natively constructed present thought for any uncommon event including birthdays, commemorations, occasions, and Father's Day. You'll discover examples for men and young men of all ages including babies, youngsters, and grown-ups.

#Pattern 1: Little Man Scarf

The strong shades of this exemplary striped scarf example makes this the perfect example for men and young men of any age. Red and blue are average boyish hues that you can't turn out badly with; even children will appreciate wearing this custom made scarf. You could likewise tweak the look of this scarf by utilizing two of his most loved hues. Utilize the shades of his most loved games group or pick his secondary school or school hues for an example he can wear to football games. It's an immortal plan that will never go out of style.

#Pattern 2: Da Beard Hat

You don't need to waste time at the shopping center scanning for the ideal custom made blessing thought for him; this exceptional knit cap example is certain to be a hit! It's a particular outline that he will totally cherish. This free sew example is a definitive grand slam of man specialties. It's intended to keep his head warm, as well as his face also. He will need to wear when he goes to football games, while he's scooping snow, and notwithstanding when he's just running errands around town.

#Pattern 3: Sports Lapghan

If your child, beau, spouse, or father is a self-broadcasted "games gentleman," then he's going to cherish this free knit afghan design. This sewed afghan is one of the best free examples to stitch for men in light of the fact that you can totally modify it to coordinate his most loved group. Besides, it's fast to work up so it makes an awesome a minute ago blessing thought. Offer this to him for his birthday, Christmas, Father's Day, or on the grounds that.

#Pattern 4: Manly Ripple Afghan

The red and dark shades of this free stitch afghan example makes this the ideal example for any man hollow. Swell afghans are a simple and engaging outline component to make and look incredible in any house. It's an extraordinary cover for him to utilize in the event that he gets icy sitting in front of the TV or playing computer games.

Straightforward Sweater for Him: This is an ageless sweater will be an incredible expansion to any man's closet. The basic style of this fantastic team neck sweater makes this an awesome alternative for all intents and purposes any event including birthdays, occasions, or simply regular wear. Utilize any shading tweed yarn that you think he may like best.

#Pattern 5: Al's Dickey

If your gentleman isn't an immense fanatic of scarves or massive winter sweaters, this free knit example is an incredible choice. It's basically a rectangular piece that is worn around your neck to keep icy air from blowing specifically down his shirt. This is a brisk and simple example to finish and it would make an incredible a minute ago blessing thought for the Christmas season. This dickey is a standout amongst the most flexible free examples to knit for men that you can discover. Indeed, you could even sew one for yourself; then both of you could be twins! Not all man specialties are entirely for men just.

Chapter 4 – Popular Baby Cocoon Tunisian Patterns

Did you realize that a considerable measure of infants touch base amid the month of September? Couples have a good time more around the merry Christmas like Christmas and New Year's, henceforth the September notoriety of child of landings. Other well known months are June, July and August. Numerous individuals appreciate having summer babies so they can arrange birthday parties outside and appreciate the warm climate. With hopeful folks come child showers!

We have assembled a spectacular accumulation of case examples only for you! Figure out how to stitch a percentage of the cutest and most surprising examples.

#Pattern 6: Crochet Cocoon

At the point when child is first conceived, you need to keep all of him pleasant and warm, including the most essential part, his head. These sets make extraordinary child shower blessings to give. The Crochet Cocoon, Hat and Booties set (appeared) is one that every single new mother will simply love. The knit cap and sew booties will keep the infant decent and warm when he's alert, however then you can swaddle him in his new cover for snooze time. Infants need a considerable measure of things in the initial couple of months, so why not run with a set?

#Pattern 7: Baby Cocoon Animal

Have you seen a case for child that resembles a creature? These free examples are so slick and genuinely new since I haven't seen them around much, yet. The Owl Baby Cocoon (appeared) is one of the cutest plans ever. This charming little owl is worked in rounds verifying that toward the end of each round it is slip sewed shut all through the whole stitch design. What's awesome about these child knit examples is that you can pick any hues you wish. On the off chance that you don't have a clue about the sexual orientation of the infant then unbiased hues like green and yellow are the best approach. Something else, this Owl Cocoon would look awesome in either pink or blue. You can even modify the look and add somewhat more flare to the cap and add pom poms to the little ears for a fun look.

#Pattern 8: Unexpected Baby Cocoon

What's your most loved thing to stitch for child? In the event that we haven't persuaded you to make one of these super charming covers yet, then simply hold up a touch longer to see what's in store for you next. Expect the surprising with regards to planning your own particular examples. This fantastic Mermaid Cocoon (appeared) is one of my top choices. Dress your infant young lady in this flawless example and even utilize it as a photography prop for her first photographs. How would you stitch something like this? All things considered, this example is worked in rounds utilizing the half twofold knit join and the back post single sew fasten. Every piece is worked independently while the mermaid top and tiara are really worked in columns!

Chapter 5 – Popular Crochet Fun Patterns

Can you trust we at last endured the icy winter months? In spite of the fact that this winter wasn't exceptionally chilly, at any rate in the Chicagoland region, despite everything I anticipate the hotter climate every season. Furthermore, with that warm climate comes all the really bright things in life, as butterflies and blossoms. Snatch a snare and some brilliantly hued yarn and make some stitch blossom designs. How about we have some butterfly stitch fun, too with this DIY eBook. Download this astonishing spring eBook today and figure out how to knit blooms and butterflies. Knit butterfly examples can be so much fun, particularly on the off chance that you work with various hues or even a variegated yarn.

#Pattern 9: Crochet Flower Pattern

Crochet blossom examples are one of my most loved things to sew at whatever time of year. While you're packaged up beside the chimney you can work up any free knit blossoms to include as extras for your winter gear. Make a little flower example to adorn a cap or even a coat. When you figure out how to knit blooms you can basically make any kind of blossom you wish. The perfect thing about spring is that you can improve your home with free stitch bloom examples and even butterfly sew designs. Rather than purchasing a bunch of blooms you can sew your own. The Double Flowers are anything but difficult to stitch, as well as you can transform them into a delightful strand of festoon to light up your home. Free knit bloom examples like these are fun in light of the fact that you can utilize numerous stitch hues to make your strand.

#Pattern 10: Crochet Buttery

You'll truly adore the butterfly stitch design on page 18. The Flutter By Butterfly Dishcloth is so flawless. It has a tad bit of that 3D look to it, while it's still practical as a dishcloth. I for one wouldn't utilize this butterfly sew design as a dishcloth. I would attempt to get imaginative with it and use it as a fun embellishment. In the event that utilized with light pastel hues I think these would look charming swinging from the roof of a tyke's room. Another thought you can utilize this outline for is a table enhancement. Fold up the wings a smidgen so they can seem, by all accounts, to be taking off the table. This is an extraordinary sample of level knit butterflies, yet there are likewise the amigurumi designs. Huge amounts of butterfly stitch fun can be had with 3D butterflies or 1D.

Chapter 6 – DIY Crochet Blanket Patterns

At the point when the winter season hits, the first things I snatch for are my stitched covers. What's more, when the late spring season hits, unfortunately, the first things I get for are my sewn covers, yet just when the cooling is impacting. Do you see a typical subject here? I adore wrapping myself from head to toe in delicate yarns, so when I see knit cover examples for learners, I hop on them like there's no tomorrow. When I initially figured out how to stitch a sweeping I utilized worsted weight yarns as a part of three sew hues regardless I utilize them right up 'til the present time.

#Pattern 11: Blanket for Kids

Birthdays showers are incredible reasons to sew a cover for a tot. These souvenirs can bring numerous recollections for the little child accepting such a brilliant blessing. In spite of the fact that children don't generally understand the significance of things until they're more established, they'll most likely welcome it over the long haul.

#Pattern 12: Crocheted Throws

It can be not the same as different afghans in light of the fact that they have more brightening examples and are some of the time shorter than covers you use to twist up in. In the event that you simply need somewhat additional solace and style in your home, however, work up one of these extraordinary sew tosses for tenderfoots.

Chapter 7: DIY Crochet Bag Patterns

In case you're searching for something extravagant for a decent event then you'll cherish the decisions of grasps that we have, yet in the event that you're searching for a regular sack then we have recently the thing, as well. We're giving the knit sack designs, you should do nothing more than get your yarn and snares and have at it.

#Pattern 13: The Mesmerizing Messenger Bag

It is genuinely astounding! Knit pack examples like this are celebrated in the sew hues that you pick, yet the example itself is simply staggering. This carefully assembled sack is trendy and spacious and can hold every one of your assets. A pleasant included touch is the discretionary strap agent, so make certain you look at this one!

#Pattern 14: The Pretty Purple Purse

It is worked in a rich purple shading to pass on for. This is a lovely sack design that you can treat yourself with. It's an easygoing looking sack that uses the puff fasten giving it that pleasant surface. The strap is sufficiently long to be worn as a cross-body sack. In case you're searching for effortlessness, then this is your go-to.

#Pattern 15: The Crochet Clutch

It is an adorable knit plan on the grounds that you can adorn it with pretty much anything. This specific DIY grip pack is adorned with two catches, however you can likewise include blossoms, sequins or appliques. This is a basic knit design that can be worked up rapidly in single stitch; the example comprises of just 32 columns.

Conclusion

Since you know how to make crochet patterns you can simply ahead and make every last one in this eBook. Rather than purchasing so as to flush cash down the can a Tory Burch, a Coach or a Fendi tote, sew your own! These outlines are choice and in the event that you make one yourself, it'll be a great deal more incredible. In case you're made a beeline for the workplace, to a wedding or to an outside occasion, we have quite recently the patterns for you.

Tunisian Crochet Patterns

Introduction

Tunisian crochet, also known as Afghan crochet, is a little bit different from your regular crochet. It still has a lot of the basics; you use hooks and yarn to create things from patterns. But there are also some differences that make Tunisian crochet much easier to pick up and learn. Let's get started with a quick look at some of those differences.

Chapter 1 – The Differences Between Tunisian and Regular Crochet

If you've taken a look at crocheting you've probably written it off as something complicated and time consuming to learn. While that's not entirely true it is hard to look past the intimidating nature. Crochet patterns don't make any sense at all unless you know what you're doing. That's also kind of true for Tunisian crochet. You'll still be dealing with patterns that you have to understand. But you can still get into Tunisian crochet more easily than you could crocheting thanks to the differences between the two.

One of the key differences is the size of the hook. Tunisian crochet is a sort of blend between crocheting and knitting. Though you don't need to know how to knit before you go into Tunisian crochet. What is meant by this is that the hook is longer than the hook in regular crochet. It actually looks a bit like a knitting needle with a hook on the end for crocheting.

Another difference, and the key one that makes it easier to learn Tunisian crochet, is the number of different stitches in a pattern. In regular crocheting there are lots of different stitches. There's the stitch, the double stitch, the treble stitch, the half double stitch, and the list goes on. You also have to turn over every so often. The really difficult things are so difficult because you have to know how to do everything before going into them. This isn't the case with Tunisian crochet.

Tunisian crochet only has five different things to remember. There's the regular chain stitch (characterized in patterns as ch), yarning over (YO), stitches (Sts), skipping (sk), and the slip stitch (Sl St), no double or treble stitches or anything inbetween. Crocheting has so many acronyms and stitches you need a glossary to keep up with them all.

The final major difference between the two is that there is no need to turn your work with Tunisian crochet. One row of Tunisian crochet is made up of two parts. There is the forward pass, which is where you pick up stitches onto the hook, and the reverse pass. The reverse pass is where you work them off the hook. These two bits go together to eliminate the need for turning over as long as you keep the right side of the yarn facing you. A pattern will usually write both passes as one row. Some other patterns won't. So always double check your pattern to make sure you understand it properly.

Those are the three major differences that make this kind of crocheting easier. It does limit what you can do however. Regular crocheting can be used to make all kinds of things but Tunisian crochet needs to be focused around smaller projects. You can make some bigger things but they take longer and are more complicated. This guide is going to focus on the small and easier things. With that said let's take a little deeper look at Tunisian crochet.

Chapter 2 – Getting Started With Tunisian Crochet

If you've worked with crocheting, or know the basics, you'll have an easier time picking up Tunisian crochet. Crocheting begins with a foundation chain and so does Tunisian crochet. With the Tunisian version you need to make a whole foundation row with a forward and return pass. The foundation row is almost always the same style too no matter what pattern or stich you use. It's all about what you do after that basic stitch.

To get started with Tunisian crochet you need to start with a slip knot and a chain stitch. To practice working your basic foundation row make a chain stitch of fifteen chains and go from there. The chain needs to be the same length as the amount of stitches you're going to work with. For example if you're working with ten stitches then your chain needs to be ten chains long. Fifteen is a basic and easy number to work with so use that as your practice.

To start working with your foundation row and working the forward pass start by inserting your hook into the second chain from the hook. That's how things work in regular crocheting too. You almost always ignore the first chain from the hook.

After inserting the hook into the chain you yarn over, which is pulling the yarn over the hook, and then pull up the loop you've made. After that you should have two loops on your hook. You need to keep the loops on the hook at all times. You also need to repeat this step for every chain on the hook. So by the time that you've finished you should have fifteen loops on your hook. That's another major difference between crochet and Tunisian crochet. You keep the loops on the hook. That's why the Tunisian crochet hook is so much longer.

Now it's time to work on the return pass of your foundation row. The return pass goes from left to right. Remember to not turn your work. You're doing this so that you don't have to turn anything over. To start the return pass begin by yarning over, and then pull through the first loop. Then you yarn over again and this time pull through two loops. This is the process you repeat for the rest of the row. You go through two loops at a time for the return pass and stop when you have one loop left. That's your first foundation row down!

This is when you start the first row. What you're working on now is actually a very basic swatch pattern that has you repeat the first row. So when you're done with this row just repeat it until you're satisfied.

Row one has vertical bars that are created from the foundation row. Remember to count them to make sure that you have the same number of bars as you do stitches. You also need to remember to use the last bar at the end.

To start the first rows forward pass skip the first vertical bar and insert your hook into the second one. Yarn over and pull up a loop to get two loops on your hook.

Keep up that pattern until you go through every bar and have fifteen loops on your hook.

Now it's time to work the return pass. Yarn over and pull through the first loop.

You'll only pull through the first loop at the beginning of the return pass. Then you yarn over and pull through two loops. Keep doing that until you have only one loop left, as you did before. Then you have another fifteen vertical bars. Just keep doing that until you're happy with the size of the swatch.

There's one very simple pattern down and one crucial skill learned. Let's now take a look at some others.

Chapter 3 – Advanced Techniques

As easy as Tunisian crochet is it isn't all just simple stitches and foundation rows. There are other things you need to know. One skill you definitely need to know is how to finish your work when you're done.

When the time comes to finish your work you start by completing the return pass on the last row of the pattern. You can fasten off similar to what you do in regular crochet, which is tightening everything up and then cutting the yarn, or you can do something fun by making a neater edge using slip stitches. To make a neater edge insert the hook under second vertical strand, bypassing the outside edge.

Pull the yarn through both loops of the hook and repeat that action along the row and you'll have made a neat little slip stitch to give your product a more polished look. It looks a lot better than just fastening off and makes the pattern a little more unique.

Another little advanced trick to know how to do is switching colors. Changing the color is needed in some patterns. You can also use it on a single color pattern to add some stripes for a bit of colorful flair. You can also use this technique to switch yarn if you find yourself running out. Whether you want to change colors or switch to a different ball of yarn here is the technique for how to do it.

If you're changing color to create solid stripes in your pattern then you need to change for the start of the forward pass. That means you pick up the new color at the end of the last reverse pass. Just hook in the new color at the end, as you would do with regular crochet. Fit it through the loop and you'll have yourself two solid blocks of color. That's also how you swap yarn of the same color. You'll have two solid blocks of the same color so no one will be able to tell that you switched yarn.

There's another little trick you can do when it comes to swapping colors. You could create two solid blocks of color, and there's nothing wrong with that, but what if you wanted to do something a little more? If you change color at the beginning of the reverse pass, rather than the end, you get an entirely different effect. All you have to do is work the forward pass in the old color, then pick up your new color at the start of the chain in the reverse pass. This makes the old color sort of fold over the new color and create an almost tunnel like effect that helps avoid some issues with the way the color stripes look, as well as adding a unique flair to your project.

There plenty of other little things you can do to add some fun to your project. There's one last one that we'll look at before moving on to some patterns for you to try. The last little advanced thing to show you is how to make a cross stitch.

Begin by chaining an odd number of chains for your foundation row. We recommend seventeen but any odd number will do. You might want to stick to the basic fifteen you've been doing until now. Remember the foundation row will almost always be the same so you don't need us to tell you how to do that again.

To start with the cross stitch skip the first and second vertical bars of your forward pass and instead insert the hook into the third bar. Then you yarn over and pull up a loop, giving you two loops on your hook.

Now, and this is where it gets a little complicated, you need to work into the second bar that you just skipped. That's why you skipped it. There's no need to turn your work or do anything fancy. Just bring the hook back and insert it into the second bar. Yarn over and pull up a loop, giving you three loops on your hook. You should be able to see already that you've made an ever so tiny cross stitch.

You just need to do that all the way across, like you did for the basic stitch. Remember to skip one bar and work on the one after, and then go back through the bar you skipped. That gets the stitches to cross over.

Now it's time to work the return pass. Work from left to right, as you always do on the return, and yarn over and pull through the first loop on the hook. For the rest of the pass you yarn over and pull through two loops, as you did before. Then you just repeat row one until you get the amount of rows you need. After a few rows you'll be able to really see the cross pattern and how great it looks.

Now that you know the basics of how to do Tunisian crochet it's time to take a look at some actual patterns for you to try at home. We're focusing on kid friendly ones. You might even want to teach your kids how to do some Tunisian crochet to give them a hobby. The length of the hooks might make it a little tricky for a small child to pick up but they can definitely give it a good go with a little help.

Chapter 4 – Basic Patterns

In the interests of making things a little easier for you the patterns will be written out properly. It's important to learn how to read them properly when you look online or in magazines for patterns of your own. If you know how to read crochet patterns then you'll know how to read Tunisian ones. If you don't then it's all about the acronyms. It was already shown earlier how the different stitches are written out in a pattern. A regular pattern uses those acronyms and numbers to condense what you have to do into a few lines.

Before you proceed there are two more techniques for you to know. The Tunisian Knot Stitch (TKS) and the Tunisian Full Stitch (TFS). The Knot Stitch is done by skipping the first loop to start with. You might notice that the vertical bars in your pattern go up into the horizontal bars, then back down the other side. To do the Knot Stitch you insert your hook between these two vertical bars under the chain. Then you yarn over and pull a loop.

The Full Stitch is pretty similar in that you skip a loop. Instead of going through the vertical bar though you insert your hook under the horizontal bar, between the vertical bars. Make sure that you don't touch the vertical bars when doing this. Then you yarn over and pull up a loop as before.

Anyway, here are some basic patterns for you to try at home to make great gifts for your kids.

1. Wrist Warmers

We'll start with something every kid needs at some point; wrist warmers. These wrist warmers should end up being about six and a half inches long and two inches tall.

The materials you're going to need for this pattern are three different colors of medium weight yarn, a 5.5mm Tunisian crochet hook, a yarn needle, and a pair of scissors.

The gauge isn't very important with this pattern but to give you an idea 7 rows should be about 2 inches thick. The pattern makes two of the warmers, or enough for one kid, and is laid out below.

Row 1: Start by chaining ten with your first color. If you chain ten and it doesn't look tall enough you can chain a few more. Just remember to chain the same amount further down the line. Change to the second color in the last chain and simple stitch starting from the second chain from the hook, then in each chain across. Change to the third color at the beginning of the reverse pass, then change back to the first color in the last simple stitch of the reverse pass.

Row 2: Simple stitch in the second stitch from the hook and in each stitch across. Switch to your second color at the start of the reverse pass. Then switch to your third color at the last simple stitch of the reverse pass.

Row 3: Simple stitch in the second stitch from the hook and in each stitch across. Switch to your first color at the start of the reverse pass. Then switch to your second color at the last simple stitch of the reverse pass.

Row 4: Simple stitch in the second stitch from the hook and in each stitch across. Switch to your third color at the start of the reverse pass. Then switch to your first color at the last simple stitch of the reverse pass.

After that you need to repeat rows 2-4 seven more times at the least. Or just keep going until the wrist warmer is large enough for you. Then move on to row five.

Row 5: Slip stitch in the second stitch from the hook and in each stitch across. All you have to do after that is just finish off.

To make your button you need to use this pattern:

Round 1: Chain two then five sc in the second chain from the hook.

Round 2: Use 4 sc in the same chain, overlapping your previous round. Then finish off.

The strap is pretty easy. To do that you just have to chain six and then finish off.

To finish off the wrist warmers properly sew a button to one end of the wrist warmer and then sew the strap to the opposite end.

2. Miniature Hat Ornament

This great little hat is the ideal decoration for a Christmas tree, or just a wonderful little project for you to have a go at. The finished size of the hat is about 1 and three quarter inches across and high. You're going to need nine yards of worsted weight yarn, an I hook (that's 5.5mm) and a yarn needle. The gauge should be about four stitches for an inch but gauge isn't overly important here.

Here's the pattern:

Row 1: Chain sixteen and then skip the first chain. Pull up the loop through the back bump of each stitch so you have sixteen loops on your hook. Then yarn over and pull through one loop. Yarn over then pull through two loops and repeat that until only one loop is left.

Rows 2-8: Skip the first vertical bar. Insert the hook from the front to the back between strands of the next vertical bar. Yarn over and then pull up a loop. Repeat that across. To return you yarn over and pull through one loop. Then yarn over and pull through two loops until one loop is left.

Row 9: Skip the first vertical bar then insert the hook from the front to the back between strands of the next vertical bar. You yarn over, and pull up a loop, then repeat that across. To return just yarn over and pull the loop through all the other loops in the row, going one or two at a time. That's how you gather the crown of the hat. Finish off and then pull tight.

To finish you turn so the wrong side is facing and whipstitch the vertical edge closed. If you've done it right the bottom edge should flip up naturally. Secure the yarn to the inside of the crown and turn the right side out, and make a loop about three inches high. Knot the yarn near the crown, secure the yarn inside of the hat, and weave in all the ends. There you have it; one tiny little hat.

3. Tunisian Scarf

One common item that's made with crocheting is a scarf. Here's a look at just one of the many kinds of scarves you can make with Tunisian crocheting. Or, indeed, any kind of crocheting.

You're going to need 7 skeins of wool and a size J (6 mm) Afghan crochet hook.

Remember Afghan crochet is just another way of saying Tunisian crochet. The gauge is that 14 stitches comes to about 4 inches.

To get started you need to work your foundation chain. For this pattern you need to chain 42 stitches. When you've made your foundation it's time to work with row 1.

Forward Row 1: Insert your hook through the space between the vertical strands, then yarn over and pull a loop through the hook. Insert the hook into the next space, yarn over, and pull the loop through onto the hook. Repeat that until you get to the last space, which needs to be skipped. Instead you insert your Afghan hook into the chain stitch at the edge. Pull the loop through onto the hook.

Return row 1: Chain one stitch, yarn over, and pull the loop through the next two stitches on the hook. Repeat until you get to the end, ending with one loop on the hook.

Forward row 2: Insert the hook into the second space, yarn over, and pull the loop through onto the hook. Insert the hook into the third space, yarn over, and pull the loop through onto the hook. Repeat that to the end of the row, including the last space. Insert your Afghan hook into the chain stitch at the edge, pull the loop through onto the hook.

Return row 2: Just do the same thing you did for the first return row. Then you just repeat these steps until the scarf is as long as you want it. The original pattern calls for 70 inches but that's way too long for a kid.

Now it's time for the finish.

This time when you do the first forward row insert the hook into the first space, yarn over, and pull through two loops on the hook. Repeat this until the end when you should have one loop left on the hook. Then you cut the yarn and pull through the remaining loop.

With the right side facing you, as you should for Tunisian crochet, join the yarn and make a single crochet into each stitch along the edge you're going to bind off.

Cut the yarn and pull through the remaining loop. Repeat that for the cast-on edge and then weave in all the ends and block how you want to finish completely.

4. Faux Knit Headband

This headband is great for keeping your kids heads warm and it's as soft as it looks.

You need two colorways of worsted weight yarn, a size J Tunisian crochet hook, and a yarn needle. Safety pins will help but aren't necessary. There isn't much of a gauge in this pattern either. Just keep going until it's the right size. You want to make one that's a few inches short because the yarn does stretch.

To begin with make a foundation chain nine stitches long using your first color.

Row 1: Work your forward pass in the first color. Drop the first color at the end and work your way back using the second color.

Row 2: Work the forward pass in the second color. Drop the second color at the end and work your way back using the first color.

Just repeat that until the headband is as long as you need it to be. When you finish the last row use a slip stitch in each stitch across.

When the headband is the right size it's time to finish it up. Cut the yarn, but leave a long trail of about ten inches long. Thread your yarn needle (you can also use a tapestry needle for this step) and stitch the two ends together. Weave in the ends and turn the headband right side out and you're good to go.

5. Crochet Beanie

Another common crocheted item is hats. This is one of the many kinds of hats you can make with Tunisian crochet.

You need one skein of soft wool, a size I Afghan hook, and a yarn needle. The gauge is that nineteen rows of nineteen stitches should give you a 5 inch square.

Row 1: Your foundation row needs to be a chain stitch of 36. Skip the first chain and pull up loops in the back bump of the other chains. Close by yarning over and pull through one loop on the hook. Yarn over and pull through two loops on the hook until you reach the end.

Row 2: Skip the first vertical bar. Working with a Tunisian full stitch insert your hook under the next 23 horizontal bars. Pull up a loop in each, giving you 24 loops on the hook. Close it by following the previous closing steps.

Row 3: Skip first vertical bar and first horizontal bar. Use a Tunisian full stitch and insert your hook under the next 23 horizontal bars, pulling up loops in each. Follow the same closing instructions.

Row 4: Skip first vertical bar. Working as for a Tunisian full stitch, insert the hook under the first horizontal bar and pull up a loop. Still working as for a

Tunisian full stitch, insert hook under the next 16 horizontal bars, pulling up loops for each. Close the same as before.

Row 5: Skip first horizontal and vertical bars. Working as for Tunisian full stitch, insert hook under the remaining horizontal bars, even the ones from row 2-4. Pull up loops in each one too. Working as for Tunisian knot stitch, pull up a loop in the last vertical bar, giving you 38 loops on the hook. Close by yarning over and pull through one loop on the hook 7 times. Yarn over and pull through 3 loops on the hook 8 times. Yarn over and pull through 3 loops on hook. Yarn over and pull through two loops repeatedly until done.

Bind off by skipping the first vertical bar. Then, working for TFS, slip under each horizontal bar across. Then cut off the remaining yarn. With the yarn needle and about 18 inches of yarn seam the last row to the foundation row. Weave the yarn loosely along the edges of each row at the top of your hat using a different piece of yarn. Cinch gently to draw the hole together and sew it together to maintain the closure. Weave all the ends in securely and flip the hat "inside out" to finish.

6. Tunisian Crochet bookmark

This is a handy little bookmark for both kids and adults to enjoy their favorite books with.

You will only need a small amount of yarn. You'll also need a size G hook. You also don't need to worry about a gauge.

The foundation chain needs to be ten chain stitches long.

Row 1: Insert the hook into the second chain from the hook. Yarn over and draw up a loop. Insert the hook into the next chain, yarn over, and draw up a loop. Repeat until done.

Row 2: Insert hook under the second vertical bar of the previous row. Yarn over and draw up a loop. Insert the hook under the next vertical bar, yarn over, and draw up a loop. Repeat until done.

Row 3-38: Repeat row 2. At the end of row 38, with just one loop left, fasten off and sew in the end. You have a small little rectangle that makes an ideal bookmark.

7. Tunisian dishcloth

This is more one for kids to make than one made for kids, but here's a simple little pattern for a colorful dishcloth

You need 1 ball of white worsted weight cotton, 1 ball of pink worsted weight cotton, a size G Tunisian crochet hook, and a yarn needle.

Row 1: Use the white cotton to chain 25. Bring up a loop in each chain across. Yarn over and pull two loops up on the hook. Repeat that until back at the start.

Row 2: Insert the hook in the hump just above the next vertical bar. Bring up a loop. Insert the hook into the next vertical bar. Bring up a loop. Repeat that across and then finish as you did before.

Row 3-17: Repeat row 2. Then fasten off the white cotton.

Now to work on the perimeter.

Round 1: Join the pink cotton in the top right corner on row 17 sc. Chain 2 sc in that corner. Sc in each stitch going across, sc, chain 2, sc in the corner. Sc in each row down the left side. Sc, chain 2 in the next corner. Sc in each stitch across the bottom. Sc, chain 2, sc in the next corner. Sc in each row up the right side. Join it together using a slip stitch in the first sc you made.

Round 2: Slip stitch into the first chain 2 sc, chain three, dc, chain 2, 2dc in the same sp. Dc in each sc across. 2dc, chain 2, 2dc, in each chain 2 corner sp. Dc in each sc across. Repeat that around. Join with a slip stitch to the top of chain 3. Fasten off the pink cotton.

Round 3: Join the white in the same stitch as the slip stitch. Chain one. Sc in each next dc. 2sc, chain 1, 2sc in next chain 2 corner sp. Sc in each dc across. 2sc, chain 1, 2 sc in the next chain 2 corner sp. Sc in each dc across. Repeat that around. Join with a slip stitch into chain 1. Fasten off and then weave all the ends into the back of the work to finish.

Let's move on now to some more advanced patterns.

Chapter 5 – Advanced Patterns

In this chapter we'll be taking a look at some harder patterns. As long as you're familiar with the terminology and what you're doing you should be able to do these patterns.

8. Tunisian Crochet Cellphone Bag

Do your children have cell phones? If they do you can use this design to create a handy little bag for them to keep it in.

You need some size ten cotton thread in green and greensh grey. Or just two colors that fit well together. A 3.5 mm steel crochet hook. A sea shell bead, and some Velcro fastening finish the list.

To make the body use a double strand of green to chain 18 + 2. Use a basic Tunisian stitch on these 18 chains for 44 rows. Then fasten up.

The flap is a little more complicated. Join a double strand of greenish grey at the beginning of the last row and work on sc in each stitch across. Then turn.

Row 2: chain three, dec over next two sc, 1 sc in each sc across to the last sc. Then dec over the last two and turn.

Row 3: Chain 2, 1 sc in each sc across to the end. Turn.

Then you repeat row 2 and 3 until 2 sc remain. Pass the thread through both and fasten off.

For the strap you knit an I-cord using one strand of green and one strand of grey. You do this by using a pair of double pointed 3mm needles, cast on 3 stitches. Knit across. Slide the stitches across the needle to the right edge and, bringing the thread to the right and behind the work, knit across again. Keep that up until the strap is as long as it needs to be and cast off the three stitches together to finish.

Finish the bag properly by sewing the sides together by using a weave stitch. Use the grey to crochet a row of sc along the margins of the flap. Attach the seashell bead to the top of the flap. Then sew the I-cord and Velcro fastening in place.

9. Tunisian Stitch Neck Warmer

This great little neck warmer is idea for keeping your loved ones necks warm in the cold weather.

You need two colors of medium weight yarn, a size I crochet hook, a yarn needle, and a pair of scissors. The gauge is that 7 rows should equal 2 inches.

Use the green yarn to chain 20, or as wide as you'd like the neck warmer to be.

Row 1: Work a simple stitch in the second chain from the hook, and in each chain across.

Row 2-53: Work the simple stitch in the second stitch and in each stitch across

Row 54: Work a simple stitch in the second stitch and in each stitch across. This time change to brown yarn in the last simple stitch.

Row 55-74: Work a simple stitch in the second stitch and then each stitch across.

Row 75: Work a slip stitch in the second stitch and then in each stitch across. Finish off.

To make the button (and you need to make two) just follow this pattern.

Row 1: Use the green yarn to chain 4, slip stitch in the forth chain from the hook to form a loop.

Row 2: Work ten sc in the loop.

Row 3: Work ten sc in the loop, overlapping the previous row.

Row 4: Work eight sc in the loop, overlapping the previous one again, and finish off.

To make the button strap, and again you need to make 2, use this pattern.

Row 1: Chain 15, then slip stitch in the first chain to form a loop, then finish off.

Use a yarn needle to sew the buttons onto the brown end of the neck warmer, and the button straps onto the green end.

10.   Afghan Stitch Coaster

It's a small thing but a coaster can go a long way and makes for a fun small project and handmade gift. This pattern also features the long single crochet. To do this insert the hook into the stitch, yarn over, and draw a loop through to have two loops on the hook. Yarn over again, draw through both loops on the hook. These are really just regular single stitches but worked in a row that isn't the regular working row.

You need white and green worsted weight wool and a size G Tunisian crochet hook.

Row 1: Use the white wool to chain 14, draw up a loop in the second chain from the hook. Draw up a loop in each remaining chain. Yarn over and draw through the one loop.

Row 2-12: Draw up a loop in each vertical bar to get 14 loops on your hook. Yarn over, draw through one loop.

Don't fasten off right now.

Now to work the border.

Row 1: Use the soft white to chain 1, sc evenly around the entire coaster base (use the pattern sc, chain 1, sc) in each corner stitch. Now you fasten off.

Row 2: Join the green yarn in any stitch you want. Sc in some of the places you placed the single stitches in row one, working the singles as you go. Sc in each sc, with three sc in each corner.

Fasten off and you're done.

11. One Skein Scarf

Scarves are nice but they can use up a lot of wool. Here's a pattern that uses only one skein of wool. This pattern uses the Tunisian double crochet. Just yarn over, slide the hook from right to left under the post of the stitch, draw up a loop, yarn over, and pull through two.

You need one skein of homespun yarn and a 9mm Afghan hook.

Start by chaining 15.

Row 1: With one loop on the needle, use a simple stitch across the chain and do your return row.

Row 2: Chain two (this counts as your first double crochet), then double crochet across the row. Then return as before.

Row 3: Repeat row one and two until the scarf is as long as you want it to be. When you're done bind off using sc.

Yes it really is that simple.

12. Knit headband

This headband is great for keeping you warm in the cold weather. It's pretty simple to make too. This pattern uses the special instruction "Make 1". You do this by inserting the hook knitwise through the fabric in the space between the stitches. Pull up the loop after.

This pattern works with any yarn and needle combination so find one that fits for you.

Get started by chaining 5.

Row 1: Pick up each loop across

Row2-5: Use a Tunisian knot stitch across the row

Row 6: find the centre stitch and knot stitch your way to it. Make 1, then knot stitch the centre stitch, make 1 again, then knot stitch your way across the rest of the row.

Rows 7-9: Knot stitch across the row.

Then just repeat row 6-9 until the scarf is 3.5 inches wide. Place a marker on the last increase row and measure the length from the beginning to that marker. Make a note of the measurement as "measurement A".

The total length of the headband should be about 18 inches. Remember that it's going to stretch when you put it on so it needs to be a few inches short. Double measurement A and subtract it from the size of the headband. This is measurement B and also needs to be noted. It'll be the main length of the headband. Continue in knot stitches across each row until you hit measurement B then it's time to start your decreases.

Row 1: find your centre stitch. Knot stitch across to one stitch before the center stitch. Skip that stitch and knot stitch the center stitch. Then skip the one after the center and knot stitch across the remaining stitches.

Row 2-4: Just knot stitch your way across the row

Repeat row 1-4 until only five stitches remain. Then complete one more row of knot stitches.

For the buttonhole row you need to find the center stitch again. Knot stitch across to the center stitch and skip it. Knot stitch from there to the end. On the return row you need to chain one for the skipped stitch.

Complete two more rows in knot stitches and bind off, and then fasten off to finish.

13. Ipod Hoodie

It's quite likely your kids have an iPod or iPhone. Because you use Tunisian stitches the hoodie is pretty thick and protective of whatever device they have.

You need sportweight cotton, and a size F needle.

To start with make a foundation of 14 chain stitches.

Row 1: Work your foundation row using simple stitch

Row 2: Work a row of knit stitches

Repeat row 2 until what you have is the size of your iPod and prepare to shape the collar.

The right side of the collar:

Row 1: Work a knot stitch in the first four stitches and finish as normal by leaving the rest of the row unworked. **Row 2** is an alternate to row 1 and what you do instead is work a knot stitch across while increasing between the last two stitches.

Row 3: Work a row of knot stitches

Row 4: Work knot stitches acrossing, increasing between the last two stitches

Row 5: Work a row of knot stitches

Repeat rows four and five until the number of loops is half of the number of chains you made in the first step.

Left side:

Join a separate piece of yarn into the unfinished row five stitches from the end. Work the same as you did on the right side but increase on the first two stitches, rather than the last two.

Then fasten off.

Pick up the stitch from the right side and work your way across the right side using knot stitches and across the left side.

Work in knot stitches until what you have fits up and over an iPod.

Hold the right sides together and then slip stitch the bottom, leaving an opening for the bottom port. Slip stitch up the sides.

Time to make the hood:

Chain an even number of stitches so that it fits around the opening. It should be around 18.

Work on even stitches using knot stitches for about eight rows and then decrease twice in the center of the next 2 or 3 rows.

Fold your work in half and whipstitch one side together for the top and then slip stitch the other end around the opening.

Lastly it's time to make the pocket:

Pick up a couple of stitches where you want your pocket to be and then work two rows of knot stitches. Then three rows decreasing at the beginning and end. Whipstitch the top down and you're done.

14. Kindle Cozy

Nothing like keeping a Kindle nice and warm between uses. Here's a handy little pattern to show you how.

You need two colors of worsted weight yarn and a MO-EZ hook. The gauge is that 6 rows should equal 2 inches.

You'll be using the Tunisian simple stitch for this. Start by chaining 18.

Row 1: Pick up a loop in every chain until the end (which is 18 loops) and do a basic return row on the way back.

Row 2-49: Pick up a loop in every vertical bar until the end (with 18 loops on the hook) and use a basic return row.

Row 50: Insert a hook through the next two vertical bars and pull up a loop. This is known as a decrease. Pull up a loop in each vertical bar until the last three stitches. Insert the hook into the next two bars and pull up a loop. Pull up a loop in the last stitch and use a basic return row.

Row 51: Repeat row 2.

Row 52: Repeat row 50

Row 53: Repeat row 2

Row 54: Repeat row 50.

Row 55 is the buttonhole row: Pull up a loop in each vertical bar for the first four stitches so you have five loops on the hook. Skip two bars and then pull up a loop in the remaining stitches, giving you ten loops on the hook. Return using a basic return except at the skipped stitches. With them you need to chain two and then complete the row.

Row 56: Pick up a loop in every vertical bar until the chain 2. Here you insert the hook into the space, making sure to go under the little bit of yarn made by skipping the stitch earlier. Pull up a loop and then keep pulling up a loop in the remaining bars. Use a basic return row.

Row 57: Repeat row 2

Row 58: This is the finish off row: Insert the hook into the vertical bar and pull up a loop. Pull the loop through the loop already on your hook, a slip stitch, and continue to the end of the row. If you're about to change color then finish off.

How to finish off: You need a kindle for this step. Or something the size of a kindle. Place the kindle on to the strip and then fold it over so you know where the sides meet. Hold the strip while removing the kindle to keep everything in place. Use a pin to help keep everything together. Take the second color and sc around the cozy, making sure you go through the thicknesses on both sides. It helps to start at the bottom of one side, go up and around the flap, and then down the other side. Now your kindle will always be nice and warm.

15. Knit stitch hat

We're finishing with another hat. This time it's a seamed hat that does wonders for keeping you warm.

You need two different colored sportsweight yarn, a J hook with the cable attached, and a tapestry needle.

Here's the pattern.

Chain 75 with your first color.

Row 1: With a loop on your hook, pick up each stitch across. Return your row like you normally would. Before you pull the hook through the last stitch you need to swap colors.

Row 2: Knit stitch across the row with a loop on your hook. Change the color on the last one of the return row again.

Row 3 onwards: Keep knitting across and repeating steps one and two, making sure to swap colors. Go until the piece is as long as you need it to be. Eight inches tall should give you a bit of a droop in your hat.

Decrease row 1: Knot stitch across each stitch. Yarn over on return row and pull through a loop. Yarn over and pull it through two more times. Yarn over and pull it through three. Yarn over and pull two three times, then yarn over and pull it through three. Repeat that step until you reach the end of the row.

Row 1A: Knot stich across with your second color, sliding the hook through the decreased stitches in the last return row. That ensures that they stay decreased ones.

Decrease row 2: Knot stitch each stitch across. On the return row, yarn over and pull through a loop. Yarn over and pull through two, yarn over and pull through three. Then yarn over and pull through 2 three times, and yarn over and pull through three. Then repeat that step until the end of the row once more.

Row 2A: Knit stitch across with another color, making the hook through the decreased stitches in the last return row. This will make sure they stay decreased, as before.

Decrease row 3: Knit stitch across like with the other decrease steps. On the return row, yarn over and pull through one loop. Yarn over and pull through two, yarn over and pull through three. Then yarn over and pull through 2 three times, and yarn over and pull through three. Then repeat that step until the end of the row once more.

Row 3A: Knit stitch across with another color, making the hook through the decreased stitches in the last return row. This will make sure they stay decreased, as before.

Decrease row 4: Knit stitch each stitch across. On the return row yarn over and pull through three. Repeat the yarn over step until the end of the row.

Row 4a: Knit stitch across with another color, making the hook through the decreased stitches in the last return row. This will make sure they stay decreased, as before. There's no need to change color this time though. You should have fifteen stitches by this point. Cut the yarn, leaving a long tail of the last color used.

Time to finish up!

Thread the yarn through the tapestry needle and insert the needle on the left of the piece. It needs to go through the last row. Slide the needle through every stitch and pull the work snugly. The top of the hat must be gathered.

Turn the work over with the right sides and use the mattress stitch seaming it all together. After that you can get rid of the curling by blocking it or adding a brim. Or you can just accept it. Either way your hat is now complete.

Conclusion

So there you have it. You know the differences between crocheting and Tunisian crocheting, and you know how to make some great little gifts for your kids. We hope you've found all this educational and that your experiments with Tunisian crocheting succeed. Good luck!